Jennifer Bu

CW01506914

A VICTORIAN LEGACY

Strand-on-the-Green as It Was

PORTIA PUBLISHING

First Published in 1993 by
Portia Publishing

© Jennifer Buckle 1993
All rights reserved

Printed in Great Britain by
The Short Run Print Company, Windsor, Berkshire

British Library Cataloguing-in-Publication Data
A catalogue record for this book is
available from the British Library

ISBN 1 897680 00 7

ACKNOWLEDGEMENTS

To Clifford and Charles Taylor for preparing the map of Strand-on-the-Green; the Local History Collection, Chiswick Public Library, London Borough of Hounslow for permission to reproduce the Prints and Photographs on the front cover and pages vi, 2, 6, 7, 10, 16, 31, 32, 33, 34, 36, 37, & 42.

To Eileen Tisdale and the late George Tisdale for some invaluable suggestions and lastly to my husband, Allan for his support and encouragement during a protracted period of research.

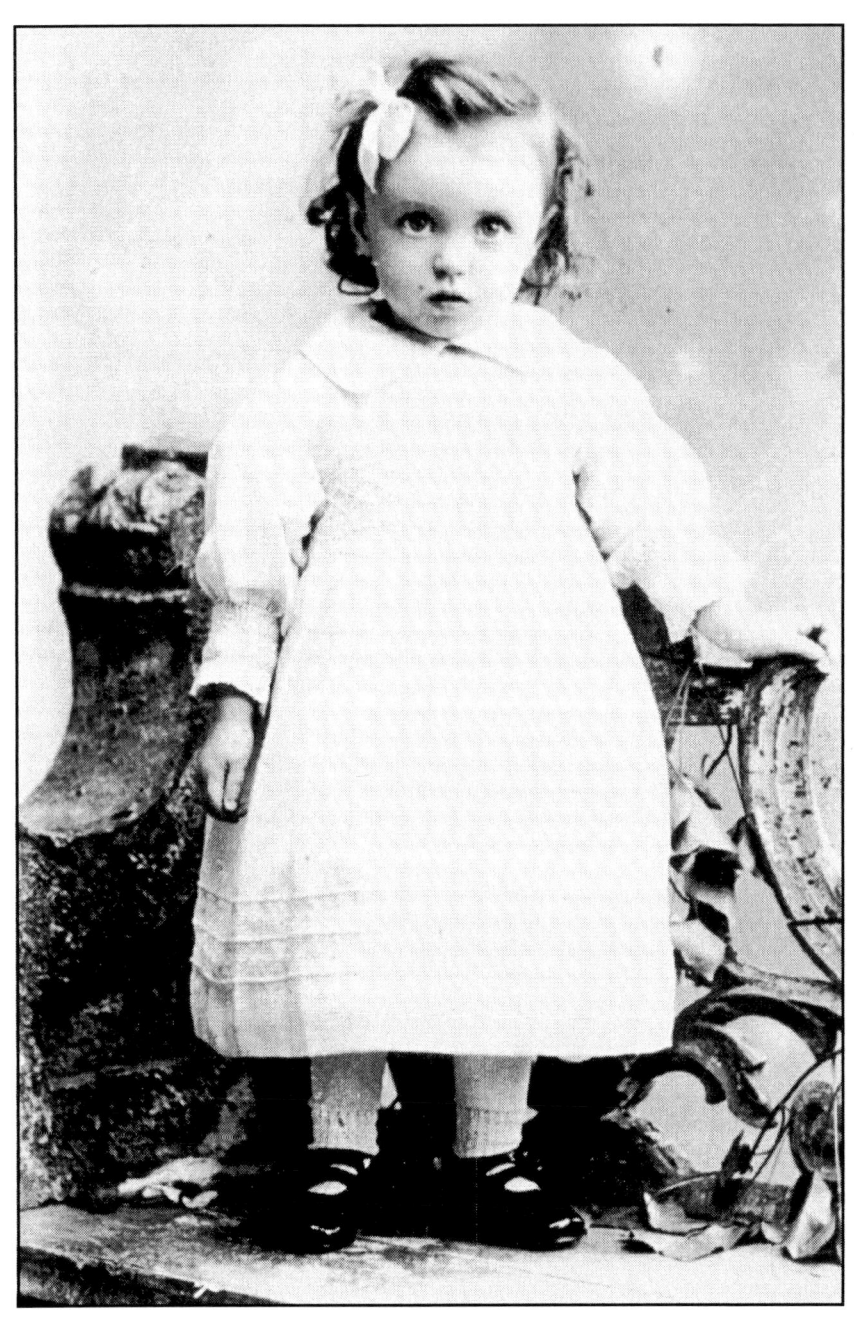

Winnie Mancey aged two 1908

IN MEMORY OF MY DEAR MOTHER
WINIFRED MAY JONES (NEE MANCEY)

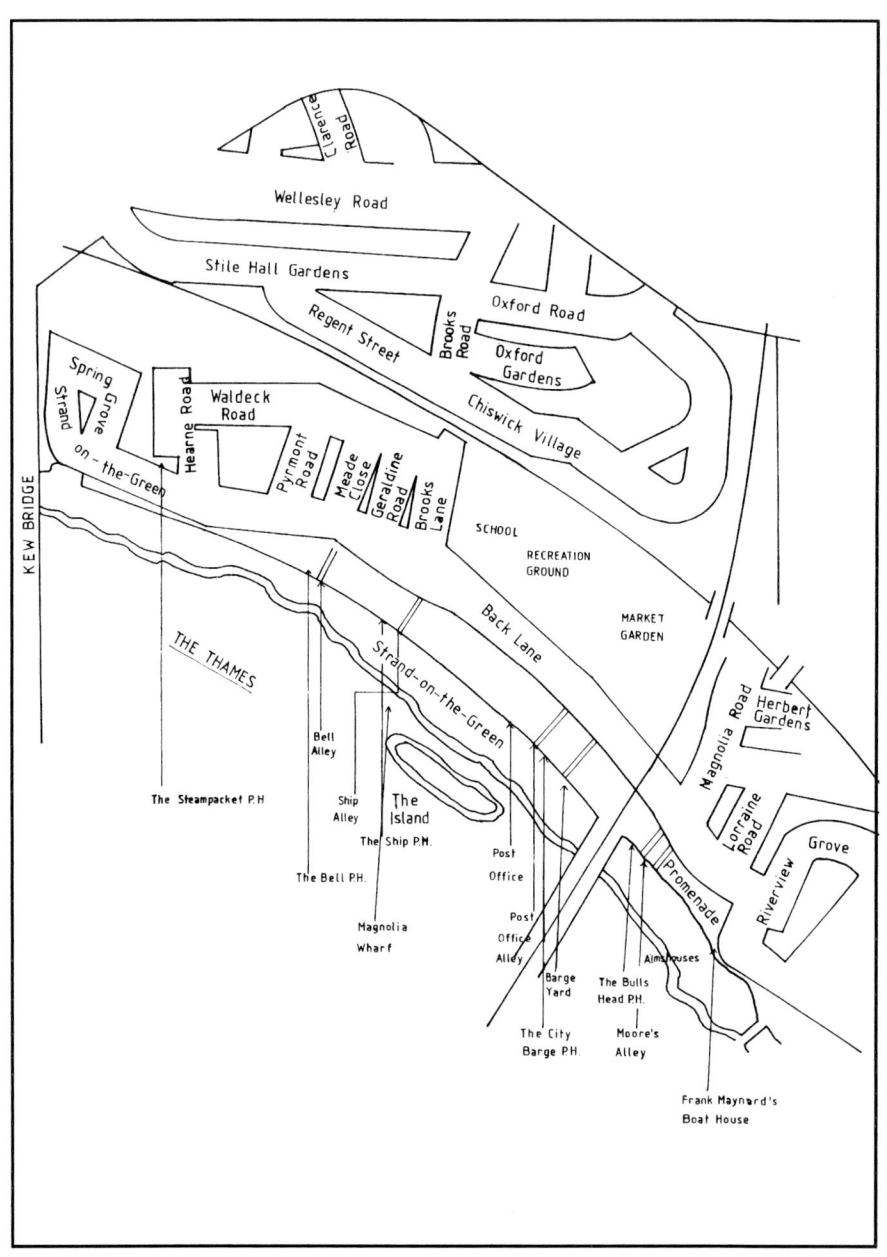

Map of the River Thames and Strand-on-the-Green

Strand-on-the-Green 1823 by W.West ARA

Section from the Panaroma of the Thames 1839

Looking down the present Post Office Alley to The Thames

Chapter 1

The Community

At the turn of the century Strand-on-the-Green was a thriving waterside village dominated by the River Thames. The Thames influenced not only the working lives of the community but in its often unpredictable ebb and flow affected the very houses in which they lived. Every house along the Strand had a tideboard at the door and sandbags ready for when an unusually high tide was not prepared to content itself with merely lapping over the tow path but tried to assault the walls of the houses themselves.

The river itself presented both excitement to the children and ever present danger to the very young who had not yet learnt to be afraid of it. In 1908 a two year old, Winnie Mancey, realised her mother's worst fears when she ran down Post Office Alley straight into the water. She was in imminent danger of being swept away by the tide when a young shopkeeper from the Post Office, Bill Winslade, saw her and with great presence of mind, used the shop blind hook to hook her out and then carried her back to her mother at 2 Post Office Alley.

Mrs. Mancey for her part was doubly alarmed since the child appeared to be covered in blood, fortunately, only the dye from her red dress. Winnie was taken home and dried and after a good nights' sleep was none the worse for her adventure, other than it left her with a lifelong dread of the water.

Once the Strand had been simply a series of connected wharves but in the 1800s it had become a continuous footpath, tides permitting.

The river itself provided a living for the menfolk mostly as Watermen or Lightermen. A "waterman" was a man navigating, rowing or working for hire a passenger boat, whilst a "lighterman" worked or navigated a lighter, barge, boat or similar craft.

In earlier days, when London Bridge was the only bridge in London over the Thames, the Waterman and his wherry were the only means that ordinary folk had of crossing the river and Watermen plied for hire up and down at the popular crossing points. By the early 1900s there were few wherries left and the term "waterman" was applied to the crew of pleasure steamers.

1905 Barge built in 1886 and owned by Smeed Dean, brickmakers, Fullers Brewery and the Pier House Laundry in the background

Lightermen however, were a thriving breed who flourished on the busy trade of the Port of London and nearer home, Brentford Dock, where the Grand Union canal and the river Brent joined the Thames. The Great Western Railway built extensive docks here so that whole fleets of barges could both load and discharge their cargo and the Thames Lighterage Company employed many men at the docks.

It is difficult to imagine now how busy the river traffic was a century ago. In 1879 there were 7000 barges registered in the books of the Waterman's Company which recorded all barges operating in the London area and the numbers were said to be increasing at the rate of 1000 a year. There were two kinds of barges, sailing barges and dumb barges (the latter operated by oars alone). The former were said to be operated by men who were skilled and careful navigators but the lightermen operating dumb barges were reviled as "A rough and reckless class......rough and disorderly".

It was said of the dumb barges that their rate of progression was so slow that they were quite incapable of getting out of the way of other river traffic and that they would bump about among the shipping and get across the bows of steamers and that the river was becoming wholly congested with them as they visited the wharves.

The waterfront at Strand-on-the-Green, like much of the river, was crowded with wharves serving numerous industries to whom the river was the primary means of transport for goods inward and outward.

For those local men not employed on the river, Fuller Smith & Turner's brewery at Chiswick also provided many men with work. Typically in 1904 a man could earn 18 shillings a week at the brewery and was allowed a generous amount of beer to drink. This perk caused problems with the men who could not hold their drink.

The men worked long hours six days a week and would take their lunch with them tied up in a fresh red and white spotted handkerchief which then doubled up as a new neckerchief for the rest of the shift.

The Cherry Blossom factory at Chiswick along with Sanderson's wallpaper factory were the other main alternatives to working on the River. "The Cherry" had started as a soap factory and subsequently converted to manufacturing boot polish.

High tides remain a risk

As the river was the main crowded thoroughfare for Strand-on-the-Green most of the roads were fairly quiet and children could safely play in the streets. Between Back Lane (later renamed Thames Road) and the river lay numerous connecting passages. Children loved to run down them and walk home along the bustling river but were always being warned not to come that way because the tides would often submerge the footpath. Some of the larger houses had their front doors at first floor level as a precaution against flood tides.

On the main road between Brentford and Chiswick there was no such peaceful scene as horsedrawn omnibuses vied with delivery vehicles and cabs creating noise, bustle and muck. Both the omnibuses and the trams were open topped. When it was raining the bottom deck would fill up and the unlucky ones would have to go upstairs. On the top deck there were mackintosh sheets attached to the seats which passengers drew over their laps for protection. The fare from Kew Bridge to Brentford was a halfpenny.

Anyone wanting to go into London would go by train but in the village few residents would have reason to go beyond Brentford or Chiswick and many would never have been further in their whole lives.

The houses were something of a mixture. Some were small and of Elizabethan origin, others grand and imposing ones dating from both the early and late Georgian period. Others still were Victorian houses, often terraced, which filled all the gaps along the waterfront and housed most of the people and their boats and sailing dinghies were moored directly in front of their houses.

1905 Boys gather outside the sweet shop by Post Office Alley

1910 Strand-on-the-Green looking East

Chapter 2

The People

The two oldest families in the village were the Pearces and the Manceys and at the close of the Victorian and the start of the Edwardian era both families were well represented by several generations all living close by one another.

The Pearce family had held a Royal Grant for fishing on the Thames with a net and eel-pots. Bommer Pearce was the last of the Strand-on-the-Green fishermen. By the early 1900's pollution of the water was such that it was hard to make a living from fishing the river but it did not stop the local boys from swimming in it.

The image of some of the Pearce family has been preserved for posterity as they sat as models for the artist Zoffany's painting of "the Last Supper" for St.Paul's Church Brentford when Zoffany lived at Strand-on-the-Green.

Jack Pearce kept the City Barge, one of a number of ancient ale-houses along the Strand-on-the-Green waterfront. Starting from Kew Bridge there was the Steam Packet, the Bell, the Ship, the City Barge and the Bull's Head. An evening's drinking might well involve going to all of these in turn to meet up with friends, relatives and neighbours.

The village was well provided with shops. Along the river front Bill Winslade ran the old Post Office at the end of Post Office Alley. The Post Office premises later became a homemade bread and cake shop and later still a drapers. The cottage next to it was a shoe repairers run by Tom Farmer who was also a verger at the Church and was generally referred to as "the Snob" as he considered himself a cut above his neighbours.

There was also a greengrocers in Post Office Alley. Otherwise along the river front there were the Pier House Laundry, several malt houses and the Thames Conservancy workshop and offices.

1895 Passengers alighting outside the City Barge

1986 The City Barge

The main centre for shops (interspersed with houses and public houses), was Back Lane where George Perkins had a market garden and greengrocery, Mr. Jenkins and Mr. Carroll both had grocery shops, Mr. Chalkley the Dairy, Mrs. Donald the Drapers, Mr. Twinn the Ironmongers, Mr. Harrison the Bakers and Mr. Levack the Butchers. There was also a recreation ground.

It was a small community and families lived in close proximity to their brothers, sisters, uncles, aunts, mothers, fathers and grandparents and it was the normal pattern of life to be surrounded, influenced and sometimes supported by an extensive family.

Some lived in style in large houses such as Zachary House and Zoffany House with an army of servants to look after the family and the house. But most lived as large families in small houses where every child had their set duties to contribute to the smooth running of the household.

Duties varied such as laying and lighting the fire in the kitchen grate for mother to cook on, blackleading the grate after use to keep it smart, or applying a whitening agent to the doorstep and even the pathway. The girls would also help to cook and clean. The boys would gather driftwood from the foreshore to supplement the supply of coal and would pump the water needed for the household from the pump outside. They were also expected to tear up folded newspaper sheets ready for hanging on the hook in the privy in the backyard, not for reading matter but as toilet paper. With an extended family unit, the privy was sometimes the only place where anyone had any real privacy.

There would always be a stockpot on the hob as a mainstay but greengrocery was brought fresh each day. The older women would go to the shop wearing sackcloth aprons and have all their purchases tipped straight into their apron to carry home.

The fishmonger used to take his cart round the streets each day with bloaters, cockles, shrimps, smoked herrings and live eels and mussels.

The muffin man called round every Sunday morning with muffins on a tin tray ringing a bell to announce his arrival and crying "Muffins and Crumpets!" as he rested the tray on a garden wall. His popularity waned somewhat after he was observed picking his nose in between handling the muffins and later on, relieving himself behind a garden wall.

Katherine Sullivan in 1895

Ellen Sullivan in 1895

Jack, the ice-cream man, went round the streets on Sunday mornings selling ice-cream and also something called "Hokey pokey" with the cry "Hokey pokey, penny a lump!". It was like an ice-cream (but not quite so nice) and when Mother could afford to buy it, the children would eat it from cornets. When she could not afford to buy it, Jack was just as likely to give the children some anyway.

In summer there was always a lavender seller on the streets of Strand-on-the-Green selling lavender at a penny a bunch.

There were plenty of churches in the vicinity to cater for the religious needs of the community with St. Paul's at Grove Park, Chiswick (adjoining Strand-on-the-Green), St. Lawrence's and St. George's at Brentford, St. Michael and All Angels at Bedford Park and St. Nicolas at Chiswick, with Non-Conformist Churches (Wesleyan and Methodist) at Brentford.

On Sundays the men would come out of St. Paul's and go straight from Church into the pub. What the vicar Nevison Lorraine thought about that is not recorded!

Chapter 3

The Manceys

The Mancey Family had been resident in Strand-on-the-Green for several centuries and at the beginning of the twentieth century there were a large number of Manceys living in the village concentrated in Back lane and along the riverfront. They lived in the houses that their fathers and grandfathers had lived in before them.

The earliest record of the Mancey's is in Chiswick Parish Register where the marriage of Robert Mancey and Elizabeth Read is recorded as having taken place on 9th January 1707.

Robert and Elizabeth's descendants can be traced for the whole of the eighteenth century and on 10th August 1804 another Robert Mancey was born. When this Robert grew up he married Sarah Collins who was a year older than him and he took his bride to live at 91 Strand-on-the-Green. He is recorded in the 1861 Census as living there with his wife and daughter, who they also named Sarah and who was then aged 19.

This Sarah also married a Robert whose surname was Levitt. He came from a wealthy family and the young couple went to live at Hounslow in a very big house.

Robert and Sarah Mancey also had two sons, Henry (born in 1840) and Thomas George (born in 1844). These sons married two sisters, Eliza and Elizabeth respectively. Both of the sons set up home in Strand-on-the-Green in Back Lane.

Number 91 Strand-on-the-Green where Robert Mancey lived would have been a large house on the river front. Rose (the second daughter of Henry and Eliza Morgan) told later generations that she remembered her grandparents as monied people who kept a carriage. Rose's mother Eliza and Aunt Elizabeth were both very good looking women who were the daughters of Rebecca Morgan and had been born at Datchet, Windsor. The sisters lived to the mid 1920s.

Elizabeth had been the cook and housekeeper to a Mr. Cecil Bovill at Grove Park, Chiswick before her marriage. Eliza is remembered as always handing out an apple and a farthing to visiting children and she also used to give the children bread and black treacle, a popular treat.

York Cottage in 1902 (now part of the City Barge)

Henry and Eliza Morgan kept a General Shop in Back Lane and had six children, the oldest being Lavinia, born the Sixteenth of July 1868 and always called 'Vine', who was very close to her sister, Rose, who was six years her junior.

In 1918 Rose married a distant cousin by the name of Gray who came from Durban but had come over to England to fight in the Great War. She went back to Durban with him but sadly he died about a year later. She then came back to England and she and Vine subsequently lived for the rest of their lives at York Cottage, their parents last house. York Cottage was next to the 'City Barge' and now forms part of it.

Rose was a Court dressmaker with apprentices and was thought to be rather 'posh'. She lived to the age of 83. Vine remained a spinster and lived to the age of 98, dying in 1966.

Thomas and Elizabeth Mancey had thirteen children, two of whom died in infancy. Of those who survived nine were boys and two were girls. Thomas and most of his sons were lightermen or watermen, the former working on tugs and barges which carried coal and other supplies from the London docks to Brentford Docks.

The two youngest sons, Sidney and Arthur, worked at the local sawmills and Arthur was subsequently the Manager of the sawmills for many years. One of the daughters, Elizabeth, married a cousin, William Mancey, who won the Doggetts coat and badge in the early 1900's. This prestigious award was for winning an annual rowing race for apprentice watermen and lightermen.

Another two sons, John and Horace, also married sisters, Honora ('Nora') and Katherine Sullivan, who were the daughters of John and Johanna Sullivan. The Sullivans were Catholics, John Sullivan having come from Cork whilst Johanna, (formerly Walsh), had been born in England.

Johanna Sullivan died whilst her daughters were young so that the eldest Nell, who was married, at first had her Father and younger sister Katherine to live with her. But Nell was inclined to be bossy so when another sister, Nora, offered to have Katherine instead, the young girl was only too pleased to move to a more congenial home. Nora looked after her younger sister right up to the time of Katherine's marriage.

Like the other Manceys they lived in close proximity all their lives. Nora survived her husband and lived to 1965 and died on the 6th October just a few days before her 96th birthday.

There were other Manceys living at William Street in the early 1900s. They were the descendants of Richard Mancey who had been born in Hampshire in 1806 and who with his brother John had moved to Strand-on-the-Green in the early part of the last century. They seem not to have been directly related to the Manceys who were descended from Robert and Elizabeth.

Chapter 4

The Young Sailor

On May 17th 1900 the British wildly and extravagantly celebrated Mafeking Day with such abandon that Piccadilly was blocked by roistering crowds as London gave itself over to a celebration that lasted three whole days.

The cause of the joy and relief was the news that the town of Mafeking had been relieved by the British Army. Mafeking, a small railway town in South Africa, had been under siege by the Boers together with the townships of Kimberley and Ladysmith.

In every street in every town in Britain the celebrations were of almost hysterical relief coming as they did only six months after the infamous "Black Week" of December 1899. This was when the British Army had been hopelessly defeated by the Boers at three successive battles in their attempts to relieve the besieged towns.

Mafeking had lain for eight months beleaguered and with the civilian population protected only by a handful of British soldiers under their commanding officer, Colonel Robert Baden-Powell, (who later founded the Boy Scout Movement). Colonel Baden-Powell had exercised the utmost ingenuity in keeping both the Boers at bay, and the spirits of the garrison town high.

The ploys which Baden-Powell used included the defenders acting out climbing over barbed wire defences (of which there were none) every time they left the garrison. This was so that the Boers watching through their telescopes would think that the town was far better defended than it was in reality. War in some areas of this campaign was slightly more civilised in one respect in that attackers and defenders of Mafeking alike observed Sunday as a day of rest. Hence the people of Mafeking were able to stretch their legs on a Sunday beyond the imaginary fortifications.

19/11/1900   H Mancey AB 28 Mu
                              Portsmout
        H.M.S. "HERO."   Hant

My Dear Brother and Sister
Jas Just a line to let you know that
I arrived safe and sound and hopin
you are quite well as it leaves me a
.... Jack what I wan
to say to you is Mate Can I
when I get married Can I & We
live with you untill such times
as I can come out of the Serv
and then I can make a Grand
Splash and I buy my home

Letter dated 19th November 1900
Horace Mancey to his brother from H.M.S. Hero

20

Katherine Sullivan at the time of her engagement

But after eight months siege the defenders had been reduced to eating horse meat. As Lady Sarah Wilson, daughter of the Duke of Marlborough (and Winston Churchill's Aunt) wired home in April 1900 "Breakfast today horse sausage, lunch minced mule and curried locusts. All well".

With the Relief Column which freed Mafeking marched the 20 year old Horace Mancey, an Able Seaman. He was part of the 940 strong force of both soldiers and sailors forming the Column. At that time sailors often found themselves fighting ashore under the command of both Naval and Army officers. The battle won, the news went winging back to England by wire where the celebrations were joyous.

In Strand-on-the-Green the celebrations were especially celebrated by the Manceys who were proud that one of their boys had been there. No-one would have been more relieved than Katherine Sullivan who was engaged to be married to Horace Mancey and who hoped to marry him on his return from the war. Katherine still lived with her sister Nora and her brother-in-law John, (who was generally known as Jack) and Horace was one of her brother-in-law's younger brothers.

Horace Mancey although still a very young man at the time of the relief of Mafeking, was a hardened veteran as far as the Navy was concerned, having joined up at the age of 13 in 1892 by lying about his age.

Horace was one of the sons of Thomas and Elizabeth Mancey and had run away to sea at the age of 13 along with his brother Walter aged 12 (there was only 10 months difference between them). Their father followed them to Portsmouth and took the younger boy back home but told Horace that as that was the life he had chosen, he had better stick to it.

Before that Horace had been a pantry boy at a big house in Chiswick where his mother had previously been employed. As the pantry boy he had many hard jobs. He had to chop firewood, get in the coal and logs and clean the knives, forks and spoons.

The silver spoons and forks were cleaned with whitening powder which was put in a saucepan with a little water, then rubbed on to the cutlery which was afterwards polished with a cloth. The knives were cleaned on a knife board which was covered with a paper like an emery paper and a brown powder was sprinkled on the board and the knives rubbed up and down on it.

The cook in the big house was somewhat suspicious of Horace and used to spy on him through the pantry key-hole. He was dismissed when he decided to retaliate by shoving a knife through the key-hole at the Cook!

The Navy taught him discipline and hard work in return for pay of 6d a day. By 16½ he was not only overseas but on active service in West Africa as part of the Navy's effort to put an end to the slave trade.

In 1897 he landed with the Benin expedition under Admiral Rawson whose orders were to try and put a stop to the slave-traders activities in the interior. Horace acted as runner for the Admiral during the ensuing battle fought in the worst possible conditions. After the battle was over he received his first medal along with the others who had taken part in the expedition. He is depicted in a painting of the battle handing a message to the Admiral.

In the Boer War Horace served in H.M.S. Sparrow based at Simonstown. H.M.S. Sparrow was "square-rigged forw'd" as steam had not yet completely ousted sail. An ordinary seaman could by then earn eight shillings and nine pence a week.

But by November 1900, just before his 21st birthday he was home again at Portsmouth attached to H.M.S. Hero. From there he wrote to his brother to ask whether following his planned wedding the following February, he and Kate could make their home with Jack until he came out of the service and could get a place of his own. Jack must have refused because in the event they were not married until 1902.

In the meantime Queen Victoria died at Osborne on the Isle of Wight on January 22nd 1901 and her body was brought back to the mainland for burial. Horace and his shipmates from the Portsmouth base H.M.S. Hero were part of the contingent of sailors who pulled the gun carriage bearing the coffin of the old Queen to her burial.

Marriage of Horace Mancey to Katherine Sullivan 20th December 1902

Chapter 5

Marriage

Horace Mancey finally married Katherine Sullivan on 20th December 1902 when she was 25 and he was 23 and on leave from the Navy. They were married at St. Paul's Church, Grove Park with many sailors and watermen at their wedding. Emerging from the Church porch they found that the horses had been removed from the shafts of their wedding carriage and instead a dozen sailors pulled the carriage through the streets to the wedding reception.

Kate had been born at Turnham Green on 1st November 1876 where her family had lived at 11 Jessops Row, Turnham Green. Kate's sister Nora had married Jack Mancey in May 1894 and they had had two children.

Kate and Horace made their home at No. 2 Post Office Alley, Strand on the Green. Post Office Alley was (and still is) a passageway leading from the River frontage by the City Barge Public House to Back Lane.

The front door of the house lead directly into the parlour with access to the living room and from there to the scullery and kitchen. Steep stairs led from the kitchen up to the two bedrooms with a door across the foot of the stairs to keep out the draught.

It was here that their eldest two children were born, Horace in 1904 and Winifred in 1906. It is said that when their eldest daughter was born at two-o-clock in the morning that a cousin went rushing to tell the new father "Its a girl Horace at two!" and he nearly had heart failure because he thought his wife had had twin girls!

Horace stayed in the Navy until 1904 and then took a job at Fuller Smith & Turners brewery at 18 shillings per week plus as much beer as he could drink. Three years later he moved his family to No. 4 Post Office Alley which was a bigger house.

From the brewery he went to work for the Thames Conservancy Board as Skipper of a dredger clearing the mud and silt where it had gradually blocked the channels. It was a job he was good at and which he also enjoyed and which daily brought its surprises as all kinds of artefacts reappeared after centuries spent on the riverbed.

Cecil Mancey

Horace Mancey (Junior)

Sidney Mancey

Of the less pleasant kind of surprises it often fell to the crew of the dredgers to recover the bodies of suicides from the river. These would be delivered up to either the Surrey or Middlesex Coroners (depending upon which side the body was recovered from) in return for a fee payable by the Coroner. As the Coroner on the Surrey side paid a higher fee than the Middlesex Coroner it was not unknown for a body to be recovered on the Surrey side having been first spotted in a somewhat different position.

The birth of another son, Cecil, on the first of January, heralded the new year in 1909. Cecil and Winifred were named after Cecil Bovill and his sister Winifred for whom Horace's mother had worked as Cook for many years (before the incident which had cost Horace his job as pantry boy).

Chapter 6

School

Strand-on-the-Green School was run for at least two generations by one Headmaster, Mr. John Mann. His wife also taught at the School and there was also an elderly (in 1910) teacher called Miss Hayter who had taught all the Mancey Brothers and Sisters in the 1880s and 90s and was still there to instruct their children in the 1900s through to the end of the Great War. The other staff were younger and one curious feature of the school system then was that the ladies in charge of classes were called Governesses rather than teachers.

A rhyme about the headmaster had been passed down the generations of schoolchildren which went:-

Mr. Mann was a jolly good man

Tried to teach you all he can

Reading writing arithmetic

Didn't forget to give you the stick

When he did he made you dance

Out of England into France

Out of France into Spain

Over the hills and back again.

The children would chant the rhyme whilst playing skipping games in the school yard. No doubt Mr. Mann had needed that stick to keep control of some of the more unruly children.

When Horace Mancey was at the school in the 1880's he was kept in one lunchtime as a punishment and was locked in the classroom. As this meant that he could not go home to dinner he knew that his mother would get to hear of it. So he climbed out of the classroom window and went home as normal! Obviously he thought the Headmaster's anger would be easier to face than his mother's.

In the 1880s parents had to pay 2d a week to send their children to Strand-on-the-Green School so that when Horace Mancey was eventually expelled from the School and had to go to Kew Green School where the fee was 3d a week, his parents were not, to say the least, pleased with him.

This did not stop Mr.Mann from welcoming Horace's children to the school in their turn. When they started school the young Mancey's were instructed by their parents not to sit next to children from William Street. This was because it was a very poor area where the children did not wear shoes and therefore might be dirty and have lice.

Horace's son Horace and daughter Winnie both did well at school work and Winnie was always top of her class and was top of the school for three years. As top girl she sometimes instructed the infants class.

At the age of 13 Winnie passed the exams to go to the Grammar School and had an interview for a scholarship but another girl eventually won it. Unfortunately Winnie suffered the fate of so many bright children at that time in that her parents could not afford to send her to the Grammar School without a scholarship so she had to leave School at 14 and start work.

Strand-on-the-Green School 1986

1893 Child on the Strand

Same view 1986

From the Illustrated Times 24th August 1867

"A short line of railways is now in course of construction ..... The works are progressing rapidly and when finished the line will form a link in the great railway system by which the metropolis will eventually be completely intersected. The line will cross the Thames by an iron bridge at Strand-on-the-Green, between Chiswick and Brentford, about half a mile below Kew Bridge. Our engraving represents this bridge in course of construction."

The same view 120 years later

Train crossing the Thames

Strand-on-the-Green after the First World War

Panorama of Strand-on-the-Green about 1902

The same view 1986

Chapter 7

The Thames

Horace Mancey's employers, the Thames Conservancy Board, had been set up in 1857. As a body they were responsible for the whole of the river from Staines down to Yantlet Creek, just above the mouth of the Medway, the Thames Commissioners being responsible for the river above Staines.

To these two bodies fell the task of keeping in repair the locks, weirs and wharves. Eventually the Thames Commissioners were disbanded and responsibility for the whole river passed to the Conservators.

In 1900 a Royal Commission was instituted to consider the best means of developing the Port of London and in 1902 it recommended that the control of the tidal river (below Teddington) should be taken from the Conservancy Board and vested in a new authority specially created to manage the affairs of shipping and the docks.

The Conservators raised strong objections, and even tried to increase their powers. but the Board of Trade was adamant, and although the fight was prolonged until 1908, in that year the Port of London Act was passed. This created the Port of London Authority to which were transferred (as from 31st March, 1909) the rights, powers and duties of the Thames Conservators in respect of the Thames below a point about 265 yards downstream of Teddington New Lock.

The struggle which had been fought out for supremacy in management of the river had been a bitter one. Lord Desborough, the Thames Conservancy chairman, had applied his considerable powers and influence in trying to maintain the supremacy of the Conservators. But when defeat finally came, he stayed on as chairman of the Conservancy Board until 1937 overseeing the modernisation and improvement of the river. He himself was a considerable river sportsman, both in rowing and swimming.

1832 The Bell & Crown Inn

Boy with boat on the foreshore

The loss of the lower reaches of the Thames from the Conservancy custody meant the loss of a considerable number of jobs on the river. The Port of London authority saw no reason to take over the men who had until then carried out the conservation and improvement work on the river and the Conservancy Board with its reduced powers sacked many of its employees.

Horace Mancey was one such and he went so far as to appeal to Lord Desborough himself to keep him on, but without success so in 1909 he found himself out of work.

Horace's life had always revolved around the sea and the river so this time he found himself a job as Pier master at Chelsea Pier in charge of Battersea, Chelsea and Hungerford Piers.

In the meantime another son, Sidney (1911) was born to Kate and Horace. Then in 1912 they moved their home from 4 Post Office Alley to "Swiss Cottage", 59 Thames Road, (as Back Lane had now become) where Horace's Uncle Percy had previously lived. Ivy, the last of their children, was born in December 1912 shortly after the move to Swiss Cottage. Horace and Kate were to continue to live there until the house was destroyed in a bombing raid in the Second World War.

1893 Lifting gear for loading barges

Horace Mancey in the First World War

Chapter 8

The War Years

Horace Mancey was still in the Naval Reserve and on August 4th 1914 (the day before War was declared), he received call up papers requiring him to join HMS "Cape of Good Hope". But his farewell party with the family lasted so long that he did not reach the ship in time before she sailed and he was posted to HMS "Glory" instead. In the event the "Cape of Good Hope" foundered and went down with all hands shortly after the opening of hostilities. The family were always thankful for that party.

Horace was away on active service from August 1914 to February 1919 on the "Glory" and after the end of the War served on The Royal Yacht, "Victoria and Albert", until his discharge in 1919. He saw service in Canada and Russia. And on March 15th 1915 was at the Naval assault on the Dardanelles and later at Gallipolli. As a gunner he did a training stint each year at the Gunnery School at H.M.S. Excellent on Whale Island.

For centuries gunners on board ships had been deafened by the incredible din of the ship's guns fired from lower decks with the noise trapped between the decks and reverberating round the hull. Horace and many of his fellow gunners inevitably became afflicted by deafness as a result of their gunnery work.

In Murmansk, it was so cold that all the sailors awoke with icicles in their beards each morning and as the sea froze they were able to exercise by playing football on the frozen sea around the ship. They were supplied with fur hats, warm boots and thick overcoats to help them to survive the cold.

At home Kate found it very difficult to manage nutritious meals for a family of six on the small allowance made to sailor's wives. Rationing had been imposed and everyone had to queue to obtain very small allowances of sausages and offal. Potatoes were very scarce at one time and families had to queue for these too and often found on getting to the head of the queue that the potatoes were the very small ones more usually given to the pigs. Even a delivery of swedes to the greengrocers would cause a queue to form, such were the shortages.

Katherine Mancey with her five children 1914

Thomas & Elizabeth Mancey 1915

Nothing much was known about nutrition, a mothers' main aim on a tight budget would be to give the family filling foods so as to prevent them from feeling constantly hungry. Porridge made a good filling breakfast or alternatively bread and dripping or potatoes if they were available. Bread, cheese and broth were usual for the lunchtime meal (which was always referred to as "dinner") and tea and toast for tea with perhaps a rice or suet pudding. Sunday dinner would be the best meal of the week with meat such as mutton and the leftovers would supplement Monday's fare.

Kate made soup with bones from the butchers adding carrots, turnips, onions and dried peas or lentils and would also make dumplings to extend the soup a bit further. The only bread available tasted disgusting and the margarine too left a lot to be desired. As there was very little sugar available they used condensed milk to sweeten tea and other drinks.

One Saturday morning Kate sent her eldest girl to get some groceries and gave her a ten shilling note to pay for them. Ten shillings (fifty pence) represented the greater part of the family's weekly income. Then suddenly German Airships (Zeppelins) appeared overhead. Kate sent someone running after Winnie to bring her back home. When the child returned she handed the ten shilling note back to her mother. Kate screamed at her "The Germans are here we won't need that now" and threw the note away.

The children were as terrified as their mother and imagined that the Germans were marching in the streets and were going to imprison them all. However, once the all clear siren sounded the first thing Kate said was "Where is that ten shilling note?!"

The nearby railway bridge became a prime target for the Germans who tried to blow it up and in fact they got very near Kew Bridge during one raid and damaged a row of shops and a market place.

During the war bread was 8d (old money) for a 2 lb. loaf. In the old coinage 1 old penny = 0.42 new pence, 12 old pence = 1 shilling, 1 shilling = 5 new pence and 20 shillings = £1. An old penny was further divided in that 2 halfpence (½d) equalled 1 penny and 4 farthings (¼d) also equalled 1 penny.

1902 Women talking near the Post Office

River front shops around 1893

Milk was 1½d per pint, butter one shilling per lb. and 8 eggs cost sixpence. Sugar was 2d per lb., coffee from 1d per lb., cheese from 6d per lb. Flour was 1¼d per lb., cabbages 1d or 2d each. Potatoes were ¼d per lb., carrots, onions and turnips 1½d per lb., suet 8d per lb. A mixture of carrots, onions and turnips was called "pot-herbs".

Jam was 5d per lb., cocoa two shillings per lb., bacon 7d per lb., currants 3d per lb. and raisins 4d per lb. Rice was 3d per lb. and tea from 1 shilling per lb. Tea was stored in large canisters labelled with a number to indicate the blend. Those who could afford it would ask for their own blend to be made up from several of the numbered canisters.

Oranges and Bananas were 1d each. Fish cost from 4d per lb. Vinegar cost 2d per pint. Meat was from about 6d per lb., when it was available. Sausages were 6d per lb. (beef) and 8d per lb. (pork).

Wages were from about one pound to two pound per week and the rent of the Mancey's cottage was seven shillings and sixpence week.

The family would take a jar to the grocer for jam, pickles, or a jug for vinegar or milk, and could buy half a pound of broken biscuits for 2d. When a customer bought a loaf of bread the baker weighed it and then would give them a small bun to make up the correct weight.

Clothes at this time cost 6d a pair for socks whilst stockings were a shilling. A pair of shoes cost ten shillings. An average dress would be five to ten shillings. A coat cost fifteen shillings to a pound. A hat two shillings, an apron 6d, whilst a blouse was two shillings and sixpence.

Soap was 3d per bar (1.lb). Coal was one shilling and sixpence per hundred weight. Cotton was a penny a reel and elastic and tape a penny for about 2-3 yards. Blacklead was 1d a lump. Cherry Blossom shoe polish was made at Chiswick and it cost 1d, or 2d for the larger tin.

When buying items at a haberdashery counter if the total came to an odd three farthings the shopkeeper handed over a packet of pins instead of the farthing change.

Horace Junior shortly before his death in 1915

Horace Junior with his grandparents at the gate of No. 53 Thames Road. A river barge had caught fire and Horace had helped to put the fire out. A newspaper photographer took this picture but Horace's mother was furious with him for allowing himself to be photographed without a collar.

Chapter 9

Death at Home

The womenfolk in Strand-on-the-Green suffered as all those families did who had husbands, fathers or sons away at the war. Everyone waited in dread for the knock at the door to announce another casualty of this war which they said would end all wars. At the least, women had to bring up their families and cope with crisis without the help of their husbands.

Kate Mancey was fortunate in having both her family and her husband's family around her in the absence of Horace.

Her eldest boy and girl were both helpful around the house. Young Horace, who was ten when his father went off to sea again, was a popular boy both at school and in the Church choir. In his spare time he did lots of jobs both for the Vicar and for his wife, who was an invalid, including pushing her bathchair when she wanted to go out. The Vicar and his wife, having no children of their own, became very fond of Horace and even approached his mother to see whether it might be possible to adopt him. But he was far too well loved by his parents for them to contemplate this.

In July 1915 Horace had his eleventh birthday and joined the Boy Scout movement which had been founded by the hero of Mafeking, Sir Robert Baden Powell. Scouting had become very popular amongst boys and many of Horace's school friends had joined too.

At home Horace shared a bedroom with Cecil who was still only six but thought it wonderful to share with his elder brother.

When Horace suddenly became ill in November it was quickly apparent that there was something seriously wrong as he had a fever, shivering and vomiting in addition to a bad throat. When a skin rash appeared the doctor diagnosed scarlet fever and Horace was rushed to the isolation hospital at Brentford.

Scarlet fever was very infectious so at home his bedroom was sealed off and the keyhole and windows blocked up and the room thoroughly fumigated. The big worry was as to whether Cecil had caught the disease from his brother so the children were kept away from school.

In hospital, Horace was in isolation and his mother, when visiting him was only permitted to look through a little window at him. Horace said to her "I do feel ill Mum" as she peered through the glass at him.

When she got back home her sister Nora had been looking after the other children. Kate was just telling her about what Horace had said (without even having stopped to remove her hat and gloves) when there was a knock at the door. A man stood there.

"Mrs. Mancey?" he said. "You're wanted at the hospital".

"But I've only just come from there" Kate protested.

"Your son was taken bad just after you left" he said. They rushed round to call another sister to sit with the children and then Kate and Nora went straight back to the hospital.

When they returned it was in a cab and Winnie, who was at the gate talking to some of her friends, saw that her Mother was crying. So was her Aunt. So Winnie too burst into tears although she didn't yet know why she was crying. It was 15th November 1915 and Horace had died of scarlet fever and severe nephritis.

Kate was distraught as were Winnie and Cecil who had lost a much loved elder brother. Sidney and Ivy were fortunately too young to understand what had happened.

But it was some weeks before Horace Senior heard the news, far away in Canada. His shipmates said that his hair turned white overnight with the shock. Compassionate leave was not possible and there was little he could do to comfort his wife so far away.

The same week as young Horace died another younger boy who lived along the road, also died of scarlet fever. It was a great shock in such a close knit community already shaken by death at the Front to start losing the children too. Three weeks later Winnie's best friend died from influenza.

But the one bright spot was that Cecil proved immune to the scarlet fever germs to which he must have been subjected.

Chapter 10

Peace

The war ended at the eleventh hour of the eleventh day of the eleventh month of 1918 but it took time to organise the demobilisation of hundreds of thousands of soldiers and sailors who all had to be brought home from the various theatres of war.

Kate had word that her husband would be home in February. The family decorated both his house and the street outside to give him a heroes welcome. Kate set off for London to meet him at Waterloo Station but unfortunately in the crush of arriving troops, she missed him. So Horace arrived home to find everyone waiting for him but his wife.

The moment he realised this he turned to to go back to find her and had to be restrained for long enough to at least say "hello" to his Father and Mother who were waiting to greet him with tears in their eyes. But at last he returned home with Kate and the family was united once more.

To the two youngest children their father was a stranger and Ivy, who was only just six, was frightened by the bearded stranger and at first cried whenever he came near.

Horace would have to find new work to support his young family and it was not going to be too easy at the age of 40 when so many men, newly released from the forces, would also be looking for work.

 But the family were together again and could begin to look forward to to a new life in the years of peace ahead in a country which the politicians promised would be fit for heroes to live in.